BBQ
and All the Fixin's

BBQ
and All the Fixin's

82 OF AMERICA'S FAVORITE

BBQ RECIPES

SIMON OREN

WITH

KC BALMER-DINHOFER

Collier Books
Macmillan Publishing Company
New York

Maxwell Macmillan Canada
Toronto

Maxwell Macmillan International
New York Oxford Singapore Sydney

Collier Books   Maxwell Macmillan Canada, Inc.
Macmillan Publishing Company   1200 Eglinton Avenue East
866 Third Avenue   Suite 200
New York, NY 10022   Don Mills, Ontario M3C 3N1

Macmillan Publishing Company is part of the Maxwell Communication Group of Companies.

Library of Congress Cataloging-in-Publication Data
Oren, Simon
    BBQ and all the Fixin's / Simon Oren. — 1st Collier Books ed.
        p.   cm.
    Includes index.
    ISBN 0-02-074575-3
    1. Barbecue cookery.   I. Title.
TX840.B3074   1994   93-22437   CIP
641.5'784—dc20

Macmillan books are available at special discounts for bulk purchases for sales promotions, premiums, fund-raising, or educational use. For details, contact:

Special Sales Director
Macmillan Publishing Company
866 Third Avenue
New York, NY 10022

First Collier Books Edition 1994

Text design and composition by Flying Dutchman Production Studio.

10 9 8 7 6 5 4 3 2 1

Printed in the United States of America

A note to our readers:

When you see a smokin' flame following a recipe, a hot bit of BBQ advice follows.

Yields for some recipes are difficult to determine. However, you'll get a fair idea of the number of servings per recipe if you simply count the number of pigs at the trough.

CONTENTS

INTRODUCTION

BBQ is one of the oldest cooking methods known to humans. Through the ages, meats, fowl, and fish have been seared over the flames of open fires, smoked in shallow pits fired by smoldering peat, and charred in leaf skins in the evening embers of wood or coal campfires.

BBQ is still enjoyed throughout the world today. But in America's South, BBQ has been raised to a fine art. As a young man, I was unaware of the nuance and variety in Southern BBQ, but a taste of pulled pork led to a bite of beef ribs, and then to a plateful of slow-cooked brisket. I was hooked on BBQ!

I settled in New York with fond memories of BBQ, but little idea that this Southern sensation would change my professional life. But years later my dream of opening a New York restaurant would become a reality. And to set my place apart from the hundreds of eating establishments located everywhere in the City, I looked back to the BBQ days and found my inspiration.

Of course, I had to serve only the very best BBQ on my Manhattan menu. But what is the best BBQ? The only way to find out was to taste them all. And so began The Great BBQ Expedition.

At first the Expedition was made by air and through the U.S. Mail. I made landfalls all over the place, from the Carolinas to

Texas, the Florida panhandle to Missouri. I tasted the BBQ, venturing forkfuls and finger food in backwater shacks and local franchises. I canvassed another 350 Chambers of Commerce for the best BBQ recipes they had. Everywhere I went, every town I wrote to, the BBQ was endorsed as the best by all but a few wise souls, who'd tell me that, truly, the best BBQ was to be found in their hometowns, the next town over, or just one more day's drive through Dixie.

It was clear that a few air strikes and self-addressed, stamped envelopes were not sufficient. I'd have to take to the road myself. And so I happened into Phase 2 of the Expedition to find the most sublime, the most succulent, indeed, the best BBQ on earth.

Phase 2 was begun in 1988 with the purchase of an old bus. After considerable renovation and more than a few wrenches in the works, I set off from New York on the wide open road. Destination: Dixie's Barbecue Belt.

As I set out, the wisdom of the BBQ sages beat a dull tattoo in the back of my brain. "The best BBQ is always down the road, in the next town, over the state line . . . ." As the Expedition moved deeper into the BBQ Belt, the drumbeats became stronger and sharper. I soon realized that all the styles of barbecue I tried were the best BBQ, that each was perfect in its own delicious way.

But just what is BBQ? North of the Barbecue Belt, BBQ evokes images of cooking on an open fire or grilling hot dogs for the family out on the patio. In the Barbecue Belt, however, BBQ conjurs not so simple a picture. Instead BBQ connotes philosophy, technique, and particular ingredients—as many and varied as the backwaters, hollows, countrysides, and cities where it is cooked.

In North Carolina I sampled smoked pork that was pulled to loose-meat perfection. My father-in-law's ribs in Kansas City were slow cooked and sauced to savor. In Texas, where beef is the pillar of the pit, my taste buds were set ablaze, only to be soothed by a tall, cold beer. And the Expedition would not have been complete without some dry-rubbed baby backs and smoky succulent chicken in Memphis.

I discovered so many fantastic flavors over the course of the Expedition that I chose not to celebrate just one barbecue style in my restaurant, but rather to celebrate barbeque as a metaphor for America. And so at Brother's, I serve up all kinds of BBQ—perfect Southern BBQ—rich in smoky flavor and complemented with a variety of sauces and side dishes.

The Expedition led me to the conclusion that no one BBQ is the *perfect* BBQ. But the Expedition also revealed why all great BBQ is so truly sublime—the greatness comes from smoking. At Brother's, smoking is our finest art. We use a very slow smoking process that not only tenderizes our meats, but also infuses it with a rich hickory flavor.

At Brother's, we serve as many authentic Southern dishes as possible, but peculiar New York tastes—and some preconceptions as to what barbecue should be—has forced certain modifications in our menu. For example, as hard as I've tried to get my customers to try the real North Carolina pig sauce on pulled pork, they keep reaching for the old Texas standby—a spicy, tomato-based sauce.

In addition to pulled pork, smoked ribs, and barbecue beef, a full complement of traditional side dishes are served up at Brother's. No barbecue feast is complete without a hunk of cornbread, some hush puppies, collard greens, or some creamy mashed potatoes topped with a spoonful of velvety cream gravy, followed up with a dessert of, say, sweet potato pie or fresh peach cobbler.

BBQ is beloved by millions of Americans. It is truly grassroots food. Yet for all those who love BBQ, few know how to fix it. But it's myth that says you can't capture the true essence of barbecue at home. This book dispels that myth and is a primer for the BBQ devotee determined to create a backyard barbecue with authentic taste and trimmings.

KC Balmer-Dinhofer, the consulting chef at Brothers and co-author of this book, worked for months testing our recipes for home use. She has extensive knowledge of Southern cuisine after working for fifteen years in New Orleans restaurants and running her own catering business. A genius with a smoker, she has captured the smoky essence of Brother's fine food in recipes for use both at your backyard pit and in your kitchen.

You don't need to buy a bus and tour the Barbecue Belt to find your version of perfect BBQ. In *BBQ and All the Fixin's*, the fine art of smokin' is explained, complete with instructions for modifying your backyard grill into a world-class smoker. Also included are instructions for marinating, rubbing, and saucin' your BBQ meats and poultry. To round out your backyard feast, a variety of recipes for authentic Southern appetizers, soups, breads, biscuits, side dishes, and dessert are included, complete with a catering section for BBQ parties of five to fifty folks.

Happy barbecuing. And when you're in New York, come pay a visit to Brother's, our melting pot BBQ store in, what else, the heart and soul of the Melting Pot!

—*Simon Oren*

THE FINE ART OF SMOKIN' OF SMOKIN'

*B*arbecue means different things to different folks. But most agree that smoking is the key to succulent, tender barbecued meats.

Whether the meat is smoked, then grilled or sauced, or eaten just as is, the meat must be cooked ever so slowly in a properly ventilated smoker over chunks of hickory wood. Chunks are better than chips. They last much longer and produce a much nicer flavor. If you cannot find chunks, use wood chips. You will need to soak them in water for thirty minutes before using them and you will need to replenish your supply with a small handful about every two hours.

You can smoke with a smoker or in a covered grill, whichever you feel more comfortable using. Just remember to place the meat *away* from the fire. Smoking means *slow cooking* with the heat from smoke, not from the fire.

Using Smokers to Smoke Meats

Cooking times and temperatures will vary depending on the equipment and method you use to smoke meats. Follow the instructions that come with your smoker to make the most of your equipment. Then experiment to find BBQ perfection.

Using Grills as Smokers

If you are using a covered grill (such as a Weber) as a smoker, you will need charcoal briquets and wood. Set the briquets to one side of the grill, then light the fire. When the briquets are hot and slightly ashy, place two or three chunks of wood in the coals. If you are using wood chips, scatter no more than half a palmful over the coals. Too much wood added at one time does not produce a smokier flavor, but rather a bitter one. As mentioned above, replenish soaked chips every two hours during cooking time to maintain the much-desired smoke flavor.

Place a small, shallow pan on the opposite end of the grill to catch any drippings. Lower the cover and allow the grill to fill with smoke, about 20 minutes. Finally, arrange the meat on the top grill shelf over the pan. Close the grill cover immediately.

Trap the Smoke

Whether smoking in a smoker or on a grill, make sure the vents are closed almost all the way. This allows only a small intake of air to keep the fire going. The minimal exhaust keeps the smoke flavoring trapped inside. The heat should stay in the range of 195 to 235 degrees Fahrenheit during the entire smoking

process. Most smokers have built-in thermometers which make "BBQ life" easy. However, it is nearly as easy with a covered grill; just add four or five briquets to the pile every two to three hours, as necessary.

Once the smoking process begins, resist the urge to peek in to see how things are coming along. Use the time suggested in each recipe as a guide before you turn or baste the meat. Otherwise, you will lose heat and moisture—and that precious smoke!

BBQ Climate

If the weather is cold, your cooking time will increase by as much as fifteen minutes per pound. Experiment and adjust your cooking schedule accordingly.

With all of this in mind, you, too, can master the fine art of smokin'!

MEAT ON THE MENU

Slow smoking makes a sublime brisket . . . the low heat and long cooking time allow the meat to tenderize naturally by breaking down the marbling. Brisket is best served the same day it is cooked, so plan your cooking time accordingly.

BEEF BRISKET

One 3- to 4-pound beef brisket
Dry Rub (see page 23)
Fast BBQ Sauce (see page 20)

Rub the meat with the dry rub, coating the entire brisket well. Place it fat side up on the grill. Smoke cook it over a slow hickory wood fire (225° F) about 8 to 10 hours, turning the meat with tongs or your fingers every 2 hours. After 6 hours of smoking, baste the meat once an hour with the barbecue sauce and continue cooking until tender to the touch.

To serve, let cool slightly so slicing will be easier. Cut with the grain and serve with warm barbecue sauce.

If using a charcoal and wood fire, marinate the meat in Brisket Marinade (page 24) for 4 to 6 hours before cooking, then rub lightly with the dry rub. For a three- to four-pound brisket using charcoal and wood heat, the cooking time will be four to six hours. If using all wood, the cooking time will be eight to ten hours.

A 7- to 10-pound brisket will take 12 to 16 hours of smoking—the longer the better. Make sure the temperature remains between 175° and 225° F.

A classic Carolina delicacy. Traditionally served with a vinegar marinade—affectionately known as pig sauce—pulled pork is also superb with ketchup concoctions and other BBQ sauces. After you've pulled the pork, be sure to save the bones. They add great flavor to slow-cooked veggies or beans.

NORTH CAROLINA PULLED PORK

One 4- to 5-pound pork butt
Salt and freshly ground black pepper to taste
Pig Sauce (see page 21)

Season the meat lightly with salt and black pepper.

Smoke over a slow hickory wood fire (225° F) about 10 to 12 hours. (If combining wood and charcoal, reduce the cooking time to 5 to 7 hours.)

To serve, let the pork cool slightly. Pull it apart, working with the grain of the meat until shredded. Chop the pulled meat into small pieces (¼ to ½ inch) and marinate in pig sauce at least 1 hour before serving. Do not let the pork sit in the marinade longer than 12 hours, as the flavor will become too strong.

If you prefer Texas-style barbecued pork, add the chopped pork to hot Fast BBQ Sauce (page 20).

Serve on buns or between two slices of white bread.

SMOKED PORK CHOPS

1 cup Fast BBQ Sauce, plus extra for brushing
  (see page 20)
½ cup low-sodium soy sauce
Six to eight 1-inch-thick pork chops
Jalapeño Pepper Jelly (see page 28)

Mix the barbecue and soy sauce together in a shallow glass pan. Add the pork chops and marinate for 1 hour. Discard the marinade.

Smoke over a slow hickory wood fire (225° F) until the meat pulls away from bone, 1½ to 2½ hours. If combining wood and charcoal, reduce the cooking time to 1 to 1½ hours.

Brush with the barbecue sauce and serve immediately. Serve the pepper jelly on the side.

BBQ connoisseurs who favor fingers to forks—but prefer a pure smoke sensation to tomato enhancement—love smoked spareribs, also known in Tennessee and its environs as "dry ribs." Be sure to make enough for seconds! Allow at least one pound of ribs per person.

SOUTHERN-STYLE SMOKED SPARERIBS

Dry Rub (see page 23)
2 to 3 sides of pork spareribs, or about 6 to 8
   pounds
Fast BBQ Sauce (see page 20) or Pig Sauce
   (page 21)

Rub the dry rub vigorously into the meat, covering it completely. Smoke over a slow hickory wood fire (225° F) 5 to 7 hours. (If combining wood and charcoal, reduce the cooking time to 2 to 3 hours.)

   To serve, cut into individual ribs and brush on the BBQ sauce or pig sauce, whichever you prefer.

Spare ribs are tough to beat in a taste test, but baby backs are the caviar of BBQ, the rib eater's ultimate. Even delicate eaters can down a mess of these sweet babies. Allow about 3/4 pound per person.

BABY BACK RIBS

Dry Rub (see page 23)
4 pounds baby back pork ribs
Fast BBQ Sauce (see page 20)

Rub the dry rub into the ribs, covering them completely. Place on a grill or rack and smoke over a slow hickory wood fire (225° F) 4 to 6 hours. If combining wood and charcoal, reduce the cooking time to about 2 hours. Brush with the hot sauce.

To serve, cut the racks into 8-inch slabs. Separate the individual ribs by cutting almost through to the bottom to give your guests a head start to good eating.

Another version of
"dry ribs"—with a
glaze that'll glaze
over your eyeballs!
M-mmm, spicy good!

COUNTRY-STYLE RIBS

Dry Rub (see page 23)
2½ to 3 pounds boneless country ribs
½ cup Jalapeño Pepper Jelly (see page 28)
2 tablespoons white vinegar

Rub the dry rub vigorously into the pork ribs. Place on a grill or rack and smoke over a slow hickory wood fire (225° F) 3 to 4 hours. If combining wood and charcoal, reduce the cooking time to about 2 hours.

To serve, bring the pepper jelly to a simmer over low heat. Add the vinegar and continue simmering another 5 minutes. Brush the mixture onto the hot ribs, return to the smoker for 25 minutes, then serve immediately. Do not add the pepper jelly too early; it darkens quickly. Pass leftover sauce for dipping.

These ribs are quite meaty, so allow only ½ to ¾ pound per person.

There're more parts to a pig than shoulder, butt, and ribs. Pork sausage is especially fine when smoked and sauced.

SMOKED SAUSAGE

2 pounds kielbasa or other pork sausage

*P*lace the sausages on a grill or rack. Smoke over a slow hickory wood fire (225° F) for 1 hour.

Split the sausages lengthwise and serve with Fast BBQ Sauce (page 20), Horseradish Sauce (page 27), or over Black-Eyed Peas (page 75).

From smoke heaven . . .
use any leftovers—if
you have any—for
Smoked Turkey Chili
(page 45).

SMOKED TURKEY

One 10- to 12-pound fresh turkey or thawed
    frozen turkey
½ cup Jalapeño Pepper Jelly (see page 28)
½ cup orange marmalade

Turkey Rub
2 tablespoons dried sage
1 tablespoon ground white pepper
2 tablespoons salt
1 tablespoon hot Hungarian paprika
1 tablespoon garlic powder

Combine the ingredients for the turkey rub. Remove the giblets from the turkey cavity and save for another use.

Rinse the turkey inside and out, then pat dry. Coat the turkey well with two-thirds of the turkey rub. Sprinkle the remaining one-third on the outside of the turkey, then rub it into the skin.

Place the bird on a rack or grill and smoke over a slow hickory or mesquite wood fire (225° F) until the turkey legs move easily, 10 to 14 hours. If combining wood and charcoal, reduce the cooking time to 6 to 7 hours.

When ready to serve, mix together the jelly and marmalade and bring to a simmer over low heat. Pass separately as an accompaniment to the turkey.

This succulent poultry could cause your company to sit up and crow!

SMOKED CHICKEN

Juice of 3 lemons
4 cloves garlic, minced
1 tablespoon salt
1/2 tablespoon ground cayenne pepper
1 tablespoon freshly ground black pepper
1 tablespoon hot Hungarian paprika
1 tablespoon ground thyme
2 to 3 whole fryers or 4 to 6 fryer halves
Texas-Style BBQ Sauce (optional; see page 22)

*I*n small bowl mix the lemon juice and all the seasonings to form a paste.

Remove the giblets from the chicken cavities and save them for another use. Rinse the chickens inside and out, then pat them dry. Generously rub the seasoning paste into the chicken cavity and skin. Place whole fryers breast side up or fryer halves skin side up on the grill or rack. Smoke whole fryers over a slow hickory wood fire (225° F) until the legs move easily in their joints, about 5 to 7 hours, or smoke split fryers 4 to 5 hours. If using charcoal and wood, reduce the cooking time to 2½ to 3½ hours for whole fryers, 1½ to 2½ hours for split fryers.

Serve with the sauce, if desired.

MELTON DR 500

SAUCIN' THE MEAT

FAST BBQ SAUCE

2 tablespoons vegetable oil
¼ cup grated onion
1½ cups white vinegar
1 cup ketchup
2 teaspoon salt
1½ teaspoons freshly ground black pepper
2 teaspoons hot Hungarian paprika
½ teaspoon ground cayenne pepper
1 teaspoon garlic powder
1 teaspoon onion powder
2 tablespoons firmly packed dark brown sugar

Heat the oil in a 4-quart saucepan over medium heat. Add the onion and cook, stirring, until soft. Stir in the remaining ingredients and bring to a boil. Lower the heat to medium and cook 40 minutes, stirring frequently.

Remove from the heat, cool slightly, and store in the refrigerator for up to 1 week.

Makes enough for 4 pounds meat.

Here's a sauce that'll make your sow's ribs sit up and oink!

PIG SAUCE (North Carolina Marinade)

1 quart white vinegar
2 tablespoons crushed red pepper
2 tablespoons freshly ground black pepper
2 tablespoons salt
2 cloves garlic, minced

Combine all the ingredients in a medium-size bowl. Let stand at least 1 hour before using.

Store in the refrigerator for up to 2 weeks.

Makes enough sauce for 4 to 6 pounds of meat.

Devote a special pot to pig sauce. The vinegar tends to cure cookware and leave its flavor behind.

A sauce with a flavor as big as the Lone Star State.

TEXAS-STYLE BBQ SAUCE

¼ cup (½ stick) butter
4 cloves garlic, minced
2 onions, minced
1 carrot, minced
¼ cup white vinegar
Juice of 1 lemon
½ cup Worcestershire sauce
⅔ cup firmly packed brown sugar
½ cup black coffee
5 cups ketchup
2 tablespoons ground cayenne pepper
2 tablespoons chili powder
2 teaspoons salt
2 teaspoons freshly ground black pepper

Melt the butter in a large saucepan, then add the garlic, onions, and carrot. Cook, stirring frequently, over low heat until tender, about 10 minutes. Add the remaining ingredients and cook until thickened over medium heat, about 2 hours.

Store in the refrigerator for up to 1 week.

Makes enough sauce for 6 to 8 pounds of meat.

Meat smoked without dry rub is like the movies without popcorn. You just gotta have it! Use dry rub on pork or beef.

DRY RUB

Mix together equal parts of salt, paprika, freshly ground black pepper, and chili powder, and a half portion of ground cumin.

Store in an airtight container in a dry, cool pantry, for up to 3 months

Portions of approximately 1 tablespoon will yield enough rub for 5 to 6 pounds of meat.

A tasty, pungent marinade . . . also good if you're cooking in the oven instead of the smoker.

BRISKET MARINADE

½ cup vegetable oil
⅔ cup low-sodium soy sauce
Juice of 4 lemons
⅓ cup prepared yellow mustard
3 tablespoons Worcestershire sauce
1 tablespoon salt
1 tablespoon freshly ground black pepper
4 cloves garlic, minced
2 teaspoons dried oregano
2 teaspoons dried thyme
2 cups dry red wine

Mix all the ingredients together until well blended.

Makes enough marinade for a 3- to 4-pound brisket.

Hhhot! Try this spicy condiment with Cajun Shrimp (page 52), mix with mayonnaise for a spicy dip, or mix into Fast BBQ Sauce (page 20).

HOT PEPPER SAUCE

4 dried hot red peppers
1 teaspoon sugar
2 tablespoons fresh lemon juice
¼ cup white vinegar
3 to 4 tablespoons water

Put all the ingredients together in a nonreactive bowl. Allow the dried peppers to soften in the mixture, about 30 to 45 minutes. Then puree all the ingredients together in a blender.

Store in the refrigerator in a covered container for up to one month.

Makes about ½ cup.

 A little goes a long way. . . .

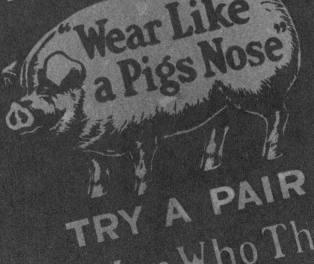

A spicy, creamy horse-radish sauce best made three to four hours before use. Serve this with Beef Brisket (page 8) or Vegetable Beef Brisket Soup (page 41).

HORSERADISH SAUCE

½ cup prepared horseradish
1 tablespoon Creole or other hot mustard
¼ cup white vinegar
¼ teaspoon ground white pepper
⅛ teaspoon ground cayenne pepper
½ cup heavy cream or sour cream

Mix together all the ingredients except the heavy cream. Let sit at room temperature for 1 hour. Blend in the cream, stirring well.
Makes about 1 cup.

Use as a glaze on Smoked Chicken (page 17), Smoked Turkey (page 16), or Smoked Pork Chops (page 10).

JALAPEÑO PEPPER JELLY

¾ cup seeded and finely chopped green bell pepper
4 jalapeño peppers, seeded and finely chopped
1½ cups cider vinegar
6½ cups sugar
One 6-ounce bottle liquid fruit pectin

*P*ut the peppers, vinegar, and sugar in a large pot and bring to a boil. Add the pectin and boil for 1 minute, stirring constantly. Remove the pot from the heat and skim off the foam. Let set approximately 5 minutes. Pour the mixture into hot, sterilized jars. Seal.

Store in a cool, dry pantry for up to 12 months. Refrigerate after opening.

Makes 6 half-pints.

Try this on smoked Baby Back Ribs (page 13).

PEPPER MINT JELLY

1 cup packed fresh mint leaves
1½ cups white vinegar
6 cups sugar
1½ cups water
¼ cup crushed red pepper
One 6-ounce bottle liquid fruit pectin

Place the mint leaves in a piece of cheesecloth and tie up. Combine the vinegar, sugar, water, and red pepper in a large pot and add the mint. Bring the mixture to a boil, stir in the pectin, and boil for 1 minute, stirring constantly. Remove from the heat, remove and discard the mint bag, skim off the foam, and let set for 5 minutes. Pour into hot, sterilized jars and seal.

Store in a cool, dry pantry for up to 12 months. Refrigerate after opening.

Makes 7 half-pints.

BETWEEN THE BREAD

Barbecue
SANDWICHES
RIBS ✶ BARBECUE PLATES

ELEGANT PULLED PORK SANDWICH

*U*se a good quality French or sourdough roll. Split the roll in half and mound 5 ounces shredded pork that has been marinated in Pig Sauce (page 21) on the bottom of the roll. Top with lettuce, tomato, and coleslaw.

CHOPPED BEEF BRISKET SANDWICH

*U*se a good quality French or sourdough roll. Split the roll in half and mound 5 ounces chopped smoked brisket that has been mixed with a generous amount of Fast BBQ Sauce (page 20). Top with lettuce and tomato. Serve with mashed potatoes, gravy, and coleslaw.

GRILLED SMOKED CHICKEN BREAST SANDWICH

*U*se a good quality French or sourdough roll. Split the roll in half and top with a smoked chicken breast brushed generously with Fast BBQ Sauce (page 20), then grilled over an open flame. Top with lettuce and tomato.

SMOKED SAUSAGE SANDWICH

*U*se a good quality French or sourdough roll. Split the roll in half and top with mayonnaise, two 4-inch pieces of smoked sausage, grated sharp cheddar cheese, lettuce, and tomato. Serve with mashed potatoes, gravy, and coleslaw.

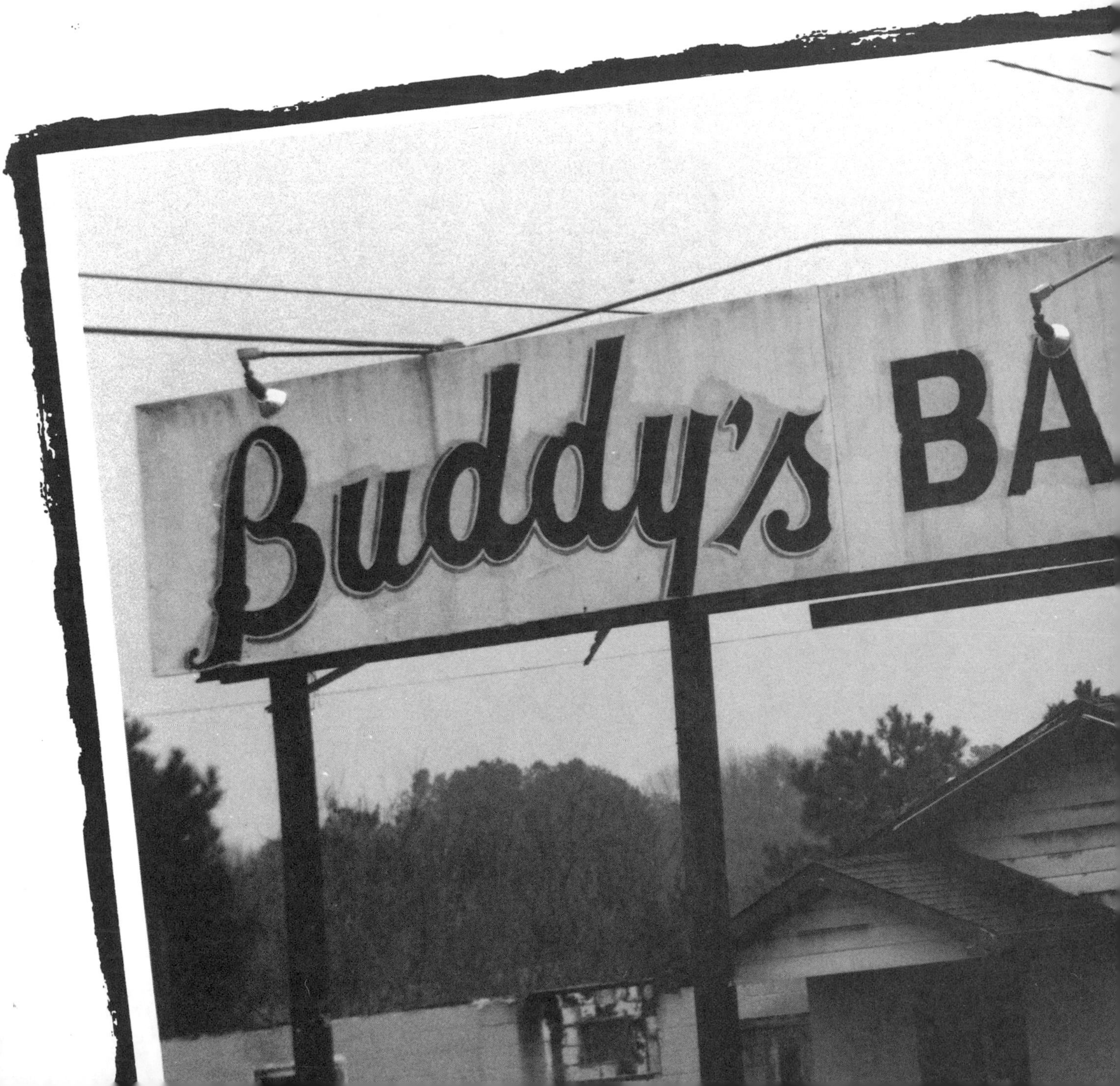
Buddy's BA

SOUPS, STEWS, AND SIMMERIN' STUFF

Porkers love root vegetables. Try 'em yourself in this tasty starter soup.

CARROT SOUP

¼ cup (½ stick) margarine or butter
2 large onions, finely chopped
4 ribs celery, finely chopped
3 cloves garlic, minced
2 pounds carrots, finely chopped
6 cups water
Salt and freshly ground black pepper to taste
Chopped fresh parsley for garnish

*I*n an 8-quart saucepan, melt the margarine. Add the onions, celery, and garlic, and cook, stirring, over low heat until golden, about 25 minutes. Add the carrots, water, and seasonings; bring to a boil. Reduce the heat to medium and let simmer 25 to 30 minutes. The carrots should be very tender. Puree, if desired.

Sprinkle with parsley and serve immediately.

Make smoked turkey stock from your smoked turkey remains . . . it makes a tasty base for pea soup. Add a ham-bone, too, to make a soup that's truly high on the hog.

SPLIT PEA SOUP

1 pound dried split peas, picked over
6 to 8 cups Smoked Turkey Stock (see page 40) or water
1 large onion, finely chopped
2 carrots, finely chopped
½ teaspoon garlic powder
Salt and freshly ground black pepper to taste

*P*lace the peas in the turkey stock, bring to a boil, and let boil until they are softened, 15 to 20 minutes. Reduce the heat to low, add the remaining ingredients, and cook over low heat 2 to 2½ hours. Mash through a strainer and serve.

Save those turkey bones—smoked turkey bones, that is!

SMOKED TURKEY STOCK

1 smoked turkey carcass (see page 16)
2 quarts water
2 carrots, quartered
1 yellow onion, quartered
8 black peppercorns
4 allspice berries
1½ teaspoons salt

*P*lace all the ingredients in a large stockpot. Bring to a boil and let cook for 15 minutes. Skim off any foam and discard. Reduce the heat to medium and simmer, uncovered, for 45 minutes. Remove from the heat, let cool slightly, then strain well. Use immediately or store in the refrigerator up to 3 days. Makes 6 to 8 cups. Freezes well.

VEGETABLE BEEF BRISKET SOUP

One 2½- to 3-pound beef brisket
6 to 8 carrots, split in half lengthwise, then quartered
4 ribs celery, split in half lengthwise, then quartered
2 large onions, quartered
4 fresh tomatoes, quartered, or 6 canned plum tomatoes, drained
6 scallions, cut into 3- to 4-inch pieces
15 sprigs fresh parsley
6 cloves
6 allspice berries
1 teaspoon dried thyme
1½ teaspoons freshly cracked black pepper
1 tablespoon salt, or to taste
3 bay leaves
Horseradish Sauce (see page 27)

*P*lace the brisket, fat side up, in a large, deep pot. Cover with the vegetables and all the seasonings, except the sauce. Add enough water to cover the meat by 2 inches. Bring to a boil, then lower the heat to medium and simmer until the meat is very tender, about 2½ to 3 hours. Do not cover.

To serve, slice the meat on the diagonal and serve with horseradish sauce. The broth and vegetables are served separately as a soup.

Beans and BBQ are a natural pair, whether served on the same plate or in courses at the same meal.

THREE BEAN SOUP

1 cup each dried pinto beans, butter beans,
and black-eyed peas (or Great Northern
beans, navy beans, and kidney beans),
picked over
3 quarts water
¼ cup (½ stick) margarine or butter
3 cloves garlic, finely chopped
2 medium-size onions, finely chopped
2 ribs celery, finely chopped
1 tablespoon Worcestershire sauce
1 bay leaf
1 teaspoon dried thyme
¼ teaspoon crushed red pepper
One 28-ounce can crushed tomatoes
½ pound smoked pork or ham, finely chopped
Salt and freshly ground black pepper to taste
Vinegar to taste
Chopped hard-cooked egg for garnish

Soak the beans overnight in 1 quart of the water. Drain. In a heavy, large pot, melt the margarine over medium heat. Add the garlic, onions, and celery, and cook, stirring, until brown. Add the remaining water, the beans, Worcestershire, bay leaf, thyme, and red pepper. Bring to a boil. Reduce the heat to medium, simmer for 2 to 3 hours, adding more water, if necessary. Stir in the tomatoes, pork, salt, and pepper. Cook 1 hour longer, mashing the beans against the side of the pot to thicken slightly.

When ready to serve, add a little vinegar (from pickled okra, page 55, is best!) and garnish with the egg.

Traditional Brunswick stew calls for critters like rabbits and squirrel to be cooked in cauldron over hardwood fires. Here's a recipe for the modern-day soup cook.

BRUNSWICK STEW

One 2½- to 3-pound chicken
1 large onion, chopped
3 ribs celery, chopped
1 quart water
One 16-ounce can peeled whole tomatoes
One 10-ounce package frozen corn
One 10-ounce package frozen lima beans
½ teaspoon garlic powder
¼ teaspoon ground cayenne pepper
½ teaspoon dried basil
Salt and freshly ground black pepper to taste

Simmer the chicken, onion, and celery in the water over medium heat until tender, 1 to 1½ hours. Remove from the heat and let cool slightly. Remove the chicken from the stock. Skim the fat from the stock, discard, and return the stock to the heat. Add the tomatoes, corn, lima beans, and seasonings. Simmer over medium heat, about 20 minutes.

Pick the chicken meat from the bones and cut into small chunks. Discard the skin and bones. Add the chicken to the simmering stock. Adjust the seasonings and cook 10 minutes longer.

For a little variation, add 1 cup diced cooked potatoes to the soup at same time you add the corn and limas.

A great way to use leftover smoked turkey (page 16) . . . if there is any!

SMOKED TURKEY CHILI

3 tablespoons vegetable oil
1 large onion, chopped
1 large green bell pepper, seeded and
   chopped
2 carrots, chopped
2 ribs celery, chopped
3 cloves garlic, minced
1 teaspoon dried oregano
One 16-ounce can crushed tomatoes
One 8-ounce can tomato sauce
2 cups Smoked Turkey Stock (see page 40)
   or water
1 tablespoon ground cumin
1 teaspoon freshly ground black pepper
1 tablespoon hot Hungarian paprika
3 tablespoons chili powder
Salt to taste
½ teaspoon ground allspice
3 cups cubed smoked turkey
1 green mango, peeled and chopped
   (optional)
2 jalapeño peppers, seeded and sliced in half

*I*n a large iron pot, heat the oil. Add the
onion, bell pepper, carrots, celery, garlic, and
oregano, and cook, stirring, over medium heat
until soft, about 5 to 8 minutes. Add the tomatoes and tomato sauce, turkey stock, and seasonings. Bring the mixture to a boil, reduce
the heat to medium, and simmer, uncovered,
for 45 minutes. Add the turkey, mango, and

jalapeños, adjust the seasonings, and continue cooking for 1 hour, adding water if necessary.

Remove the jalapeños before serving.

Try this thick and spicy combo as a hearty appetizer.

SMOKED SAUSAGE OVER BLACK-EYED PEAS

1 pound smoked sausage (see page 15), split in
  half lengthwise and cut into 4-inch pieces
2 cups hot cooked black-eyed peas
  (see page 75)

Grill the sausage or fry it in a skillet until heated through. To serve, ladle ½ cup black-eyed peas topped with 2 pieces of smoked sausage per serving. Pass hot vinegar (from pickled okra, page 55) or Creole mustard, and hot, crusty bread.

FINGER FOOD

Split the chicken wings so the "tips" get really crunchy.

CHICKEN WINGS

1 cup all-purpose flour
½ teaspoon hot Hungarian paprika
½ teaspoon garlic powder
¼ teaspoon ground cayenne pepper
Salt and ground white pepper to taste
1 pound chicken wings, split
Vegetable oil for deep frying

Special Tangy Sauce
½ cup mayonnaise
½ teaspoon ground cayenne pepper, or to taste
Pinch of salt

Mix the flour and seasonings together. Dip the chicken wing pieces into the seasoned flour, coating well.

Heat 6 inches of oil in a fryer or 3 inches in a deep skillet. The oil is hot enough when a pinch of flour sizzles in it. Add the wings to the oil, being careful not to crowd them; you may have to fry them in batches. Fry until golden. The tips take 2 to 3 minutes and the "drumettes" about 5 minutes. Drain well on paper towels.

Mix together all the ingredients for the sauce and serve it with the wings—on the side.

In snootier Southern homes, catfish may be too common for the dinner table. But, for a fix of friend food, catfish fingers, hush puppies, and creamy coleslaw make fine eating with BBQ.

CATFISH FINGERS

1½ pounds catfish fillets, cut into ½- by
   3-inch pieces
Cold milk for soaking
1½ cups cornmeal
1 teaspoon salt
1 teaspoon freshly ground black pepper
1 teaspoon ground cayenne pepper
½ teaspoon garlic powder
Vegetable oil for deep frying
Special Tangy Sauce (see page 50; optional)

Rinse the catfish under cold water and pat dry. Place in a shallow bowl and cover with milk until ready to use.

Mix together the cornmeal and all the seasonings. Lift the fish pieces out of the milk and roll them in the seasoned cornmeal until well coated. Place them on a platter to sit until all have been dredged.

Meanwhile, heat 6 inches of oil in a fryer or 3 inches in a deep skillet to 370° F. The oil is hot enough when a pinch of cornmeal sizzles in it. Add the fish pieces to the oil, being careful not to crowd them; you may have to fry them in batches. Fry until golden brown, about 5 minutes. Drain well on paper towels.

Serve with the sauce, if desired.

*Not really BBQ fare—
but a great Southern
starter for a smoky
feast.*

CAJUN SHRIMP

Vegetable oil for deep frying
1 pound medium to large shrimp, peeled and
   deveined
1 1/2 cups cracker meal
1/4 to 1/2 teaspoon ground cayenne pepper
2 teaspoons salt
1 teaspoon freshly ground black pepper
Special Tangy Sauce (see page 50)

Heat 6 inches of oil in a fryer or 3 inches in a deep skillet to 375° F. The oil is hot enough when a pinch of the cracker meal sizzles in it.

Wash the shrimp and pat dry. Mix the cracker meal and seasonings together. Dredge the shrimp in the cracker meal, shake off any excess meal, and drop 10 to 12 shrimp in the oil. Be careful not to crowd. Deep fry until golden brown, about 4 to 5 minutes. Do not overcook. Drain on paper towels.

If not serving immediately, hold in a 200° F oven for up to 30 minutes.

Serve the shrimp with the sauce on the side.

*A simple starter and a
sensational side dish
for smoked meat. Use
the hot fat from hush
puppies to cook up this
Southern staple.*

FRIED OKRA

Vegetable oil for deep frying
1 cup all-purpose flour
1 teaspoon salt
½ teaspoon garlic powder
½ teaspoon freshly ground black pepper
½ teaspoon hot Hungarian paprika
1 pound fresh okra, cut into 1-inch pieces, or
   frozen cut okra, thawed

*H*eat 6 inches of oil in a fryer or 3 inches in a
deep skillet to 375° F. The oil is hot enough
when a pinch of the flour sizzles in it.

Mix the flour and seasonings together in
a shallow bowl or pie plate. Dredge the okra in
the flour, shaking of any excess, then drop
the okra pieces into the hot oil. Be careful not
to overcrowd. Deep fry until golden brown,
about 4 to 5 minutes. Drain well on paper
towels.

Serve immediatcly.

Soups **Corona** Vegetable
Black Bean Extra WHIPPED Sweet Potatoes
CORN
zucciini

Brunswick Stew
GAZPACHO
Special Entrees

Baby Back Ribs 10.95
Smothered Shrimp 10.25
Bourbon Chicken 9.95
Blacken Black Fish 11.95
Sauteed Scallops 10.95

APP. Fried Green Tomatoes 3.75
Grilled Marinated Shrimp Salad 6.95

EXCELLENCE SINCE 1925

A great garnish for a spicy Bloody Mary. Save the spicy vinegar to pour over Three Bean Soup (page 42), Black-Eyed Peas (page 75), or Hoppin' John (page 76)!

PICKLED OKRA

2 pounds young okra pods
1 ¼ teaspoons dill seeds
25 small garlic cloves, peeled
2 ½ teaspoons crushed red pepper, or to taste
3 cups white vinegar
1 cup water
6 teaspoons salt

Wash the okra, leaving on the small stems. Divide between 5 sterilized 1-pint jars. To each jar add ¼ teaspoon dill seeds, 5 garlic cloves, and ½ teaspoon red pepper. Next, mix together in a large saucepan the vinegar, water, and salt. Boil the mixture for 5 minutes, then pour it over the okra.

Run a knife around the sides of the jars to release any air bubbles. Seal the jars. Place the jars in a large pot filled with boiling water (do not let the water cover the jars). Let the jars stand in the boiling water for 5 minutes.

Let the okra "pickle" at least 3 weeks before serving. Store for up to 6 months. Refrigerate after opening.

Makes 5 pints.

When selecting okra for pickling, never pick pods longer than 3½ inches or they will be too tough to eat.

Thin batter lets the onions "speak" to the BBQ—and be heard! Fried onions are a great appetizer as well a tasty side.

FRIED ONION RINGS

Peanut oil for deep frying
2 yellow onions, thinly sliced and separated into
  rings

Batter
¾ cup all-purpose flour
1 large egg, slightly beaten
½ cup buttermilk (or enough to make a thin batter)
½ teaspoon salt
½ teaspoon baking powder
Ground cayenne pepper to taste

Heat 6 inches of oil in a fryer or 3 inches in a deep skillet to 375° F. The oil is hot enough when a pinch of flour sizzles in it.

Mix all the batter ingredients together until smooth. Dip the onions into the batter, letting any excess drip off, and deep fry a few at a time until golden brown, 4 to 5 minutes. Drain well on paper towels.

My first fried dill pickles were served in a catfish restaurant in Maumelle, Arkansas. They make a great beginning to a BBQ . . . chased with ice cold beer!

FRIED DILL PICKLES

Peanut oil for deep frying
3 to 4 dill pickles, sliced ¼ inch thick
Plain bread crumbs
1 large egg beaten with 2 tablespoons water
Salt and freshly ground black pepper to taste

Heat 6 inches of oil in a fryer or 3 inches in a deep skillet to 375° F. The oil is hot enough when a pinch of bread crumbs sizzles in it.

Pat the pickles dry on paper towels. Dredge each slice in the bread crumbs, then in the egg wash, then again in the bread crumbs. Fry a few at a time until golden brown, about 2 to 3 minutes. Drain well on paper towels.

Hold in a shallow pan in a 250° F oven until all the slices are fried. Hold for no longer than 30 minutes before serving.

When ready to serve, sprinkle with salt and pepper. If they are salted ahead of time, they can get soggy.

BREADS AND BISCUITS

BUTTERMILK BISCUITS

3 cups all-purpose flour
1 tablespoon baking powder
2 teaspoons sugar
1 teaspoon salt
1 teaspoon baking soda
½ cup vegetable shortening, chilled
1 cup plus 2 tablespoons buttermilk

Sift the dry ingredients together in large bowl. Using a pastry blender or 2 knives, cut in the shortening until the mixture is very coarse. Add 1 cup of the buttermilk and mix quickly with a fork until the mixture is wet but not sticky. If necessary, add the remaining buttermilk. Do not beat.

On a lightly floured counter or board, roll out the dough to about ½-inch thickness. Cut out biscuits with a 1½-inch cutter or with an inverted drinking glass. Place on ungreased baking sheets and bake in a preheated 475° F oven until golden, 8 to 10 minutes. Serve hot with butter and homemade jam, or lots of cream gravy (page 71).

Makes 16 biscuits.

It's impossible to improve on a buttermilk biscuit, but some sweet milk variations offer certain pleasure.

CHEESE AND BACON BISCUITS

2 cups all-purpose flour
3 teaspoons baking powder
1 teaspoon salt
6 tablespoons vegetable shortening, chilled
½ cup grated sharp cheddar cheese
¼ cup bacon, cooked until crisp and finely crumbled
⅔ cup milk

Sift the dry ingredients together in a large bowl. Cut in the shortening with a pastry blender or 2 knives until the mixture is coarse. Cut in the cheese and bacon. Add the milk and mix with a fork until the ingredients are just combined.

On a lightly floured counter or board, roll the dough into a large circle about ½ inch thick. Cut with a floured 1½-inch cutter or inverted drinking glass into rounds. Place on ungreased baking sheets and bake in a preheated 400° F oven until golden, 10 to 12 minutes.

Serve immediately.
Makes 16 biscuits.

The name "spoon bread" seems to be a twentieth-century moniker for a Native American pudding, describing the method of eating—that is, with a spoon—instead of the character of this cornmeal delight.

SPOON BREAD

2 large eggs, separated
1 cup milk
1 cup water
1 cup cornmeal
½ teaspoon salt
2 tablespoons baking powder
1 tablespoon butter, melted

Beat the egg yolks together and set aside.

Heat the milk and water in a saucepan until almost boiling. Reduce the heat to medium and slowly stir in the cornmeal and salt to prevent lumping. Cook 5 minutes, stirring frequently. Add the egg yolks, baking powder, and butter. Remove from the heat.

In another bowl, beat the egg whites until stiff peaks form. Fold the whites into the cornmeal mixture. Pour into a greased 9-inch casserole and bake in a preheated 400° F oven for 40 minutes. Serve hot.

The perfect side for a plate of pulled pork. Hush puppies are nothing more than cornmeal dumplings—although sprinklings of scallions and seasonings are often added for variety, flavor, and fun. Confederate soldiers are said to have named these fritters. If, when cooking their mess over campfires, they heard any Yankees coming, they'd toss some golden balls to the dogs, whispering, "Hush, puppies!"

HUSH PUPPIES

1 cup all-purpose flour
2 cups cornmeal
2 teaspoons salt
2 teaspoons baking powder
½ teaspoon ground cayenne pepper
¼ cup grated onion
2 tablespoons minced scallions
4 large eggs, slightly beaten
2 to 2½ cups buttermilk
1 package dry yeast
Vegetable oil for deep frying

*I*n a large bowl, mix together the flour, cornmeal, salt, baking powder, and cayenne pepper. Add the onion and scallions and toss well.

In a separate bowl, blend together the eggs, 2 cups of the buttermilk, and the yeast. Stir into the dry mixture, using your hands to blend. The mixture should resemble a thick paste. If the mixture is too dry, add more buttermilk.

Let the batter sit at room temperature for 30 minutes. Mix well.

Heat 6 inches of oil in a fryer or 3 inches in a deep skillet to 350° F. The oil is hot enough when a pinch of the batter sizzles in it. Using a tablespoon measure, scoop heaping tablespoonfuls of batter into the hot oil. Do not crowd the pan. Deep fry until golden brown, about 4 to 6 minutes. Drain on paper towels.

Makes about 36 hush puppies.

 For a hush puppy variation known as Delta Dogs, add minced jalapeño peppers to the puppy batter.

*Pioneer cuisine—
great with BBQ,
catfish, or, for fancy
folks, prepared as
breakfast crumpets.*

CORNBREAD

2 cups cornmeal
2 cups all-purpose flour
2 tablespoons baking powder
3 teaspoons baking soda
1 teaspoon salt
2/3 cup bacon drippings or vegetable oil
2 large eggs
2½ cups milk

Sift together the dry ingredients. Put the drippings in a large bowl. Add the eggs and beat until frothy. Stir in the milk. When well blended, stir in the dry ingredients. Pour into large, greased iron skillet or heavy, ovenproof pan and bake in a preheated 475° F oven until golden, about 20 minutes.

For a smoky variation, add bits of crispy fried bacon to the batter.

FORK

FOOD

Crisp, cool, and creamy, coleslaw is great with any BBQ anytime, anywhere.

COLESLAW

1 medium-size head green cabbage, cored and
  shredded
4 carrots, grated
½ onion, finely minced
½ cup mayonnaise
1 tablespoon sugar
3 tablespoons white vinegar
½ teaspoon celery seeds

In large bowl, toss together cabbage and carrots. In another bowl, mix together the remaining ingredients to make a dressing. Pour the dressing over the cabbage mixture and toss well.

Chill 2 to 3 hours before serving.

A delicious alternative

to coleslaw.

POTATO SALAD

5 medium-size red potatoes, cubed
3 ribs celery, chopped
5 scallions, white part only, finely chopped
¾ medium-size green bell pepper, seeded and
   chopped
1 dill pickle, chopped
2 hard-cooked eggs, mashed
½ cup mayonnaise
1 tablespoon prepared yellow mustard
1 teaspoon Worcestershire sauce
2 teaspoons salt
Hot sauce to taste

*B*oil the potatoes in water to cover until tender, about 15 minutes. Drain and rinse under cold water. Drain well and toss the potatoes with the celery, scallions, bell pepper, and pickle. Mix together the eggs, mayonnaise, mustard, Worcestershire, salt, and hot sauce until smooth. Pour over the potato mixture and stir well.

Refrigerate overnight before serving.

Don't peel away flavor, eat the skin—along with a dollop of butter or cream gravy.

MASHED POTATOES

6 medium-size Idaho potatoes, quartered
¼ cup (½ stick) margarine or butter
½ teaspoon salt
½ teaspoon garlic salt
Freshly ground black pepper to taste
Hot milk

*I*n a large pot, cover the potatoes with water. Bring to a boil and let boil until tender, 20 to 30 minutes. Drain well. Add the margarine and seasonings, then mash well. Stir in hot milk and blend to a smooth, creamy consistency.

Serve hot with butter or cream gravy (recipe follows).

For Horseradish Potatoes, omit the salt, increase the garlic salt to ¾ teaspoon, and add 5 to 8 tablespoons cream-style horseradish, depending on your taste for hotness.

CREAM GRAVY

½ cup (1 stick) margarine or butter
1 cup all-purpose flour (slightly more may be
  needed)
¼ teaspoon freshly ground black pepper
¼ teaspoon garlic powder
2 cups warm milk
1 cube chicken bouillon

*I*n a heavy skillet, melt the margarine over medium heat. Immediately add the flour, stirring constantly until thickened. Add the pepper and garlic powder and mix well, continuing to stir. The mixture should brown slightly. Remove the skillet from the heat.

Meanwhile, in a 6- or 8-quart saucepan, bring the milk to a simmer. Add the bouillon cube, stirring until dissolved.

Remove from the heat and carefully stir the flour mixture into the hot milk. The mixture may bubble over. Stir well to blend and return to the heat, stirring constantly until the gravy is of the desired thickness.

An adult version of candied yams . . . but kids will love them too!

BOURBON SWEET POTATOES

2 pounds sweet potatoes, peeled and cut into
   ½-inch cubes
2 tablespoons margarine or butter
¼ teaspoon salt
1 teaspoon ground cinnamon
¼ teaspoon ground nutmeg
¼ teaspoon ground cloves
¼ teaspoon ground white pepper
1 tablespoon sugar
3 tablespoons blended whiskey
¼ cup triple sec

Grease a 2-quart casserole dish and set aside.
    Boil the potatoes in water to cover until tender, 15 to 20 minutes. Drain well.
    In a small saucepan, melt the margarine, then stir in the seasonings and sugar. Add the liquor and bring to a boil, stirring until the sugar is dissolved. Mix into the cooked sweet potatoes.
    Pour the mixture into the casserole and bake in a preheated 350° F oven for 30 minutes.

Delicious with pulled pork (page 9), country-style ribs (page 14), or beef brisket (page 8).

CORN PUDDING

1 tablespoon butter
¼ cup seeded and chopped red bell pepper
¼ cup seeded and chopped green bell pepper
2 tablespoons chopped scallions
3 tablespoons cornmeal
1 tablespoon salt
½ cup cold milk
2 cups milk, scalded
2 cups fresh corn with liquid or one 10-ounce package frozen corn, thawed, and 2 tablespoons heavy cream
2 large eggs, slightly beaten

*M*elt the butter in a small skillet over medium heat. Add the peppers and scallions and cook, stirring, until soft, 7 to 10 minutes.

In the top of a double boiler over simmering water, stir together the cornmeal, salt, and cold milk, then stir in the hot milk. Cook and stir until the mixture begins to thicken. Remove from the heat and stir in the remaining ingredients. Pour into a greased 11- by 9-inch casserole and set in a pan filled with hot water that comes about halfway up the sides of the casserole. Bake in a preheated 350° F oven until the center is firm, about 1 hour.

Serve immediately.

An alternative to potatoes as a BBQ accompaniment, also a tasty starter.

GREEN ONION CAKES

1½ cups cornmeal
¾ cup all-purpose flour
1 tablespoon baking powder
½ teaspoon salt
2 large eggs, lightly beaten
1½ cups buttermilk
¼ cup (½ stick) margarine, butter, or bacon drippings, melted
¾ cup chopped scallions, white and green parts
¼ teaspoon freshly ground black pepper, or to taste
Sour cream (optional)

*I*n a large bowl sift together the dry ingredients. Stir in the eggs, buttermilk, and margarine, mixing well. Do not beat. The batter will be a little lumpy and should have the consistency of pancake batter. If the batter is too thick, add a little more buttermilk.

Fold in the green onions and black pepper. Drop by large spoonfuls onto a greased hot griddle or skillet. When the mixture bubbles, flip to cook the other side until golden.

Serve immediately. Serve with a dollop of sour cream, if desired.

Makes 24 cakes.

Introduced by way of the Caribbean, this African dietary delight is enjoyed from Charleston to Galveston.

BLACK-EYED PEAS

1 pound dried black-eyed peas, picked over
½ pound slab bacon, cut into 3-inch pieces
4 cloves garlic, minced
1 large onion, chopped
½ cup seeded and chopped green bell pepper
½ cup seeded and chopped red bell pepper
1½ teaspoons salt
¼ teaspoon crushed red pepper
Salt and freshly ground black pepper to taste

Cover the peas with water and soak overnight (or bring to a boil, boil 2 minutes, turn off the heat, cover, and let stand 1 hour). Drain. Return the peas to a large pot. Cover with 2 quarts water and add the bacon, garlic, onion, bell peppers, salt, and red pepper. Cook over low heat until the peas are tender, adding water if necessary, about 2 hours. Season with salt and pepper.

It's good luck to eat black-eyed peas on New Year's Day, and better luck to enjoy 'em year round. This peas-and-rice dish is a Southern favorite.

HOPPIN' JOHN

1 cup dried black-eyed peas, picked over
½ pound slab bacon, cut into 3-inch pieces
2 cloves garlic, minced
1 large onion, chopped
½ green bell pepper, seeded and chopped
1½ teaspoons salt
¼ teaspoon crushed red pepper
Salt and freshly ground black pepper to taste
2 cups hot cooked rice

Cover the peas with water and soak overnight (or bring to a boil, boil 2 minutes, turn off the heat, cover, and let stand 1 hour). Drain. Return the peas to a large pot. Cover with 2 quarts water and add the bacon, garlic, onion, bell pepper, and red pepper. Cook over low heat until the peas are tender, about 2 hours. Most of the liquid should evaporate. Season with salt and pepper.

Drain all but about ¼ cup liquid from the pot. Add the rice and mix it lightly into the peas.

Serve hot.

Don't add the salt until the end of cooking time as adding it earlier will toughen the peas.

For country-style Hoppin' John, substitute 2 cups cooked diced potatoes for the hot rice.

Reserve the tasty broth—called potlikker—to sauce up leftovers.

COLLARD GREENS

3 pounds collard greens
1 cup water
1 large ham bone or bones from smoked pork
½ cup coarsely chopped onion
½ teaspoon freshly ground black pepper
¼ teaspoon ground cumin
1 teaspoon salt, or to taste
1 tablespoon white vinegar

Wash the greens thoroughly to remove all sand. Tear off the stem ends. In a 6- to 8-quart pot, bring the water to a simmer. Add the washed greens, ham bone, onion, and seasonings. When the water returns to a simmer, cover and cook about 10 minutes. Stir well, cover again, and cook over low heat until the greens are very tender, about 45 minutes. Add the vinegar and stir well.

Drain before serving.

Another way to cook

this Southern staple.

SMOTHERED OKRA

2 tablespoons vegetable oil
1 medium-size onion, chopped
1 rib celery, chopped
1 small green bell pepper, seeded and chopped
1 pound okra, cut into 1-inch pieces, or two 10-
  ounce boxes frozen cut okra, thawed
One 16-ounce can crushed tomatoes
1 teaspoon salt
1/4 teaspoon freshly ground black pepper
1/4 teaspoon ground cayenne pepper
1/4 teaspoon dried thyme

*I*n a heavy pot, heat the oil. Add the onion,
celery, and bell pepper, and cook, stirring,
until soft, about 5 minutes. Do not brown.

Add the okra and cook, stirring frequently,
until the okra is no longer stringy, 10 to 15
minutes. Add the tomatoes and seasonings.
Simmer over low heat until very tender, 30 to
40 minutes.

When the weather's too cool for coleslaw, cook up some cabbage for a warming, tasty treat.

SMOTHERED CABBAGE WITH WHITE SAUCE

½ pound slab bacon, cut into ½-inch cubes
1 large onion, thinly sliced
½ teaspoon sugar
2 small heads cabbage, cored and quartered
1 teaspoon salt
½ teaspoon freshly ground black pepper

Thin White Sauce
¼ cup (½ stick) margarine or bacon drippings
¼ cup all-purpose flour
1 teaspoon salt
¼ teaspoon ground white pepper
2 cups milk

*I*n a large, heavy pot, cook the bacon over medium heat till barely golden and most of the fat is rendered. Pour off all but 2 tablespoons of the bacon drippings, remove the bacon, and reserve for another use. Add the onion, sprinkle with the sugar, and cook over low heat, stirring frequently, until the onions are very soft and golden (the sugar will begin to caramelize the onions), about 15 minutes.

Meanwhile, slice the quartered cabbage, then add it to the onions. Add the salt and pepper, stir, and cover. Cook over low heat for about 1 to 1½ hours. Stir occasionally to prevent sticking.

To make the sauce, melt the margarine over low heat. Add the flour, salt, and pepper, and stir until well blended. Remove from the heat. Gradually stir in the milk and return to the heat. Cook, stirring continuously, until the sauce is thickened and smooth. Add the sauce to the cabbage and stir.

Serve hot.

Succotash served cold the next day makes a fine side dish, too.

SOUTHERN SUCCOTASH

¼ cup vegetable oil
5 ounces smoked pork (see page 9), finely
   chopped
1 large onion, chopped
1 cup seeded and chopped green bell pepper
2 cloves garlic, minced
One 10-ounce package frozen sliced okra
½ cup water
One 10-ounce package frozen corn
One 10-ounce package frozen baby lima beans
2 fresh tomatoes, chopped, or 4 canned peeled
   tomatoes, crushed
1½ teaspoons salt
1 teaspoon ground white pepper

*H*eat the oil in a large pot. Add the pork, onion, bell pepper, and garlic, and cook 5 minutes over low heat, stirring frequently. Add the okra and continue cooking until the vegetables are soft and the okra is no longer stringy, about 10 minutes. Add the water, corn, lima beans, tomatoes, salt, and pepper. Stir well and let the mixture simmer until the lima beans and okra are tender, about 20 minutes.

An unusual vegetable,
a distant relation to
baked beans.

BBQ'D LIMA BEANS

1 pound frozen baby limas
1/3 cup finely chopped smoked pork (see page 9)
2 cloves garlic, minced
1 cup Fast BBQ Sauce (see page 20)

Cook the beans according to the package instructions. Add the smoked pork and garlic. Place in a small casserole, pour the sauce over, and mix well.

Bake, uncovered, in a preheated 350° F oven 35 to 40 minutes.

A Southern secret made popular in the movies.

FRIED GREEN TOMATOES

1 cup all-purpose flour
2 teaspoons salt
½ teaspoon freshly ground black pepper
¼ teaspoon ground cayenne pepper
¼ cup bacon drippings
3 firm green tomatoes, sliced about ⅛ inch thick

Mix together the flour, salt, pepper, and cayenne. Heat the bacon dripping in a heavy skillet. Dip the tomato slices in the seasoned flour and fry over medium heat until golden brown on both sides. Remove and drain on paper towels, then place in a shallow pan and hold in a preheated 200°F over until all the tomato slices are fried.

Serve immediately plain or, if desired, with skillet sauce (page 85), a tomato-flavored version of cream gravy.

SKILLET SAUCE

Skillet drippings from frying tomatoes
2 tablespoons all-purpose flour
½ teaspoon salt
¼ teaspoon freshly ground black pepper
1½ cups milk

After all the tomatoes are fried over medium heat, add the flour to the skillet and stir to loosen any bits of tomato. Sprinkle with the salt and pepper. Add the milk and stir until thickened. Pour over the hot fried tomatoes and serve immediately.

STEWED GREEN BEANS

4 slices bacon, cut into 1-inch pieces
1 green bell pepper, seeded and finely chopped
1 medium-size onion, finely chopped
2 cups fresh green beans broken into 2-inch
  pieces or one 16-ounce bag frozen green beans
1½ teaspoons salt
½ teaspoon freshly ground black pepper
⅛ teaspoon ground cayenne pepper
¼ teaspoon sugar
¼ teaspoon chili powder
¼ teaspoon dried thyme
One 16-ounce can peeled whole tomatoes, drained

*I*n a heavy 4-quart saucepan, cook the bacon until almost crisp. Drain the bacon on paper towels and set aside.

Pour off all but 3 tablespoons of bacon fat from the skillet. Add the bell pepper and onion, and cook, stirring occasionally, over low heat until soft, about 10 minutes. Add the remaining ingredients. Continue cooking over low heat about 30 to 45 minutes, breaking up the tomatoes while stirring.

Sprinkle with the cooked bacon and serve hot.

Perfect with smoked meat and corn pudding.

SWEET 'N' HOT BAKED BEANS

¼ pound slab bacon, cut into 1-inch pieces
2 large onions, chopped
½ cup blackstrap molasses or firmly packed dark
   brown sugar
½ teaspoon ground cayenne pepper
2 tablespoons Creole or hot prepared mustard
   with horseradish
One 32-ounce can pork and beans

*I*n a heavy ovenproof 4-quart pot, cook the bacon until golden but not crisp. Drain on paper towels.

Pour off all but 3 tablespoons of the bacon drippings from the skillet and add the onions. Cook over low heat, stirring, until very soft, about 15 minutes. Pour in the molasses, cayenne, and mustard, and mix well. Stir in the bacon bits and beans and bake in a pre-heated 350° F oven for 45 minutes.

Not necessarily a traditional BBQ side dish, macaroni and cheese is nevertheless a wonderful accompaniment to smoked meats.

BAKED MACARONI AND CHEESE

3 tablespoons margarine or butter
¼ cup all-purpose flour
1 teaspoon salt
1 teaspoon dry mustard
½ teaspoon ground white pepper
2½ cups milk, scalded
2½ cups grated medium-sharp cheddar cheese
½ pound elbow macaroni, cooked until barely
  tender and drained
¼ cup plain bread crumbs
Hot Hungarian paprika to taste

Grease a 2-quart, oblong casserole dish and set aside.

Melt the margarine in a 2-quart saucepan over low heat. Stir in the dry ingredients and blend until smooth. Slowly pour in the milk, stirring constantly until the mixture is smooth. Continue cooking over low heat, stirring frequently, until thickened, about 10 minutes. Remove from the heat, add 2 cups of the cheese, and stir until melted.

Place the macaroni in the prepared casserole and pour the melted cheese over it, mixing well.

Mix together the remaining ½ cup cheese, the bread crumbs, and paprika. Sprinkle over the top of the casserole and bake in a preheated 375° F oven until golden, 25 to 30 minutes.

Delicious for breakfast as well as with BBQ at dinner.

JALAPEÑO CHEESE GRITS

2 cups quick-cooking grits
4 cups water
2 teaspoons salt
¼ cup (½ stick) margarine or butter
2 cups grated sharp cheddar cheese
2 to 4 jalapeño peppers, seeded and finely chopped
2 tablespoons Worcestershire sauce
2 teaspoons garlic powder
1 large egg, lightly beaten
Hot Hungarian paprika (optional)

Grease a 13- by 9-inch casserole dish and set aside.

Combine the grits, water, and salt in a saucepan. Bring to a boil and let boil about 3 minutes. Remove from the heat and add the margarine, cheese, jalapeños, Worcestershire, and garlic powder. Stir in the egg. Mix well until the butter and cheese have melted.

Pour the grits into the casserole dish and sprinkle with paprika for color. Bake in a preheated 350° F oven for 15 to 20 minutes.

Serve hot.

For those with a tender palate, try garlic cheese grits. Simply omit the jalapeños, or replace them with seeded and chopped bell pepper.

SWEET
NOTHIN'S

*The quintessential
Southern nut—
excluding, perhaps,
the Georgia peanut
(which is really a
legume)—pecans grow
in orchards throughout
the South.*

PECAN PIE

3 tablespoons butter, softened
1 cup sugar
3 large eggs
4½ teaspoons all-purpose flour
1 cup dark Karo syrup
1 cup pecan halves
2 teaspoons pure vanilla extract
One 10-inch unbaked pie shell, pricked with a fork

Cream the butter and sugar together in a large bowl. Add the next 5 ingredients, combine well, and pour into the pie shell. Bake in a preheated 450° F oven for 10 minutes, then reduce the heat to 350° F and bake until a knife inserted in the center of the pie comes out clean, about 1 hour. The pie should be a rich, deep brown color, and slightly runny when cut. Let cool completely before serving.

Serve at room temperature.

Use your favorite pastry recipe to make the pie shell, or buy a pastry mix or frozen shell at the grocery store.

Deep, dark, rich, and chunky. Make this pie the day you want to serve it . . . if you refrigerate it, it becomes so thick you can't slice it!

CHOCOLATE FUDGE PECAN PIE

3 ounces unsweetened chocolate
3 tablespoons butter
4 large eggs
1¾ cups sugar
Pinch of salt
1 teaspoon fresh lemon juice
1 cup broken pecans
One 9-inch unbaked pie shell, pricked with a fork
1 cup heavy cream, whipped to firm peaks

*I*n the top of a double boiler set over simmering water, melt together the chocolate and butter.

In a bowl, beat the eggs until frothy. Gradually add the sugar, salt, and lemon juice. Slowly add the chocolate mixture until thoroughly blended. Stir in the pecans. Pour the mixture into the unbaked pie shell. Bake in a preheated 350° F oven until the pie is flaky, about 35 minutes.

Do not chill. Cool the pie completely and serve with the whipped cream.

Similar to sweet potato pie (page 95) . . . creamy and delicious!

PUMPKIN PIE

2 large eggs
⅓ cup firmly packed light brown sugar
⅓ cup granulated sugar
½ teaspoon ground cinnamon
Pinch of ground ginger
Pinch of ground nutmeg
Pinch of ground cloves
One 16-ounce can pumpkin puree
½ cup milk
6 tablespoons heavy cream
One 10-inch unbaked pie shell, pricked with a fork
1 cup heavy cream, whipped to firm peaks

*I*n a large mixing bowl, beat the eggs. Add the sugars, spices, and pumpkin, and mix well. Slowly beat in the milk. Stir in the heavy cream and mix until well blended. Pour into the pie shell. Bake in a preheated 350° F oven until a knife inserted in the center comes out clean, about 1 hour.

Serve chilled with the whipped cream.

Like pecan pie (page 92), a synonym for "Southern dessert."

SWEET POTATO PIE

3 medium-size sweet potatoes, pricked with a fork
2 large eggs, slightly beaten
2/3 cup firmly packed light brown sugar
1 cup milk
1 teaspoon pure vanilla extract
1/2 teaspoon ground allspice
1/2 teaspoon ground cinnamon
1/4 teaspoon ground nutmeg
Pinch of salt
One 9-inch unbaked pie shell, pricked with a fork
1/2 cup heavy cream, whipped to firm peaks

Bake the sweet potatoes in a preheated 450° F oven for 1 hour. Let the potatoes cool slightly, then peel and mash well. Beat in the eggs and sugar, blending well. Slowly blend in the milk until the mixture is smooth. Stir in the vanilla, spices, and salt. Pour into the pie shell and bake in a preheated 450° F for 15 minutes. Reduce the oven temperature to 325° F and bake until a knife inserted into the center comes out clean, about 30 minutes.

Serve warm or cold with the whipped cream.

A simple pie made of unusual ingredients. Delicious after a big barbecue when you want just a little something sweet. In Tennessee, these pies are stacked in layers to make chess cake.

CHESS PIE

¾ cup (1½ sticks) butter, melted
1½ cups sugar
3 large eggs, slightly beaten
1 teaspoon pure vanilla extract
1 tablespoon cornmeal
1 tablespoon white vinegar
One 10-inch pie shell, baked at 350° F for
    15 minutes

Cream together the butter and sugar. Blend in the eggs, vanilla, cornmeal, and vinegar. Pour into the prebaked pie shell. Bake in a preheated 325° F oven until the pie is set and golden, 30 to 35 minutes.

Let the pie cool 30 minutes before serving.

Tart yet sweet—an inspired ending for a feast of pulled pork and pig sauce.

RHUBARB PIE

1¼ cups sugar
⅛ teaspoon salt
⅓ cup all-purpose flour
½ teaspoon ground cinnamon
3 cups rhubarb, cut into 1-inch pieces
2 cups sliced strawberries
2 tablespoons butter
One double (top and bottom) 9-inch unbaked
  pie shell, bottom pricked with a fork
Sugar for sprinkling

Combine the sugar, salt, flour, and cinnamon in a large bowl. Mix in the rhubarb and strawberries. Let stand about 15 minutes. Fill the pie shell with the rhubarb mixture and dot with butter. Top with the remaining crust, seal, and cut ½-inch slits into the dough to allow steam to escape during baking. Sprinkle the top crust lightly with sugar and bake the pie in a preheated 400° F oven until the crust is golden and flaky, 40 to 45 minutes.

Authentic . . . rich but tart. You can buy bottled Key lime juice in many supermarkets if fresh is not available. If you can't get Key lime juice, substitute 5 tablespoons of lime juice and 3 tablespoons of lemon juice.

KEY LIME PIE

6 large eggs, separated
One 8-ounce can sweetened condensed milk
½ cup Key lime juice
One 9-inch unbaked pie shell, pricked with a fork
¼ cup sugar

*I*n a medium-size mixing bowl, beat the egg yolks slightly. Add the condensed milk and mix well. Blend in the juice. Pour the mixture into the unbaked shell.

In a clean bowl, beat the egg whites until stiff peaks form, gradually adding the sugar to form a meringue. Swirl the meringue on the pie, making sure to seal the edges of the crust with it. Bake in a preheated 300° F oven until the meringue is slightly golden, about 30 minutes.

Cool, quick, creamy—
and delicious!

PEANUT BUTTER ICE CREAM PIE

1½ pints vanilla ice cream
2 cups creamy low-salt peanut butter
One 9-inch chocolate cookie crumb pie crust
  (see page 100)
¾ cup hot fudge topping, at room temperature
½ cup heavy cream, whipped to firm peaks
Chopped unsalted peanuts

Soften the ice cream slightly in a large mixing bowl. Beat in the peanut butter, blending well. Pour into the chocolate pie crust. Cover loosely with plastic wrap and place in the freezer until the pie is set on the outside, about 1 hour. Remove from the freezer and spread the hot fudge topping over the top. Return the pie to the freezer until firm, about 3 hours.

Serve with the whipped cream and chopped unsalted peanuts, if desired.

Do not use freshly ground or homestyle peanut butter or the oil will separate from the peanut mash in the filling.

CHOCOLATE COOKIE CRUMB CRUST

1 cup finely ground plain chocolate wafers
½ cup unsalted peanuts, very finely chopped
¼ cup (½ stick) margarine or butter, melted

*T*oss together the cookie crumbs and nuts. Place in a 9-inch glass pie plate and pour in the melted margarine. Mix well with a fork until the mixture is thoroughly moistened. Use your fingers to pack the crust firmly on the bottom and sides of the pie plate. Bake in a preheated 350° F oven for 10 minutes. Remove from the oven and let cool to room temperature before adding the filling.

For a gingery variation, substitute ginger snaps for the chocolate wafers.

Sometimes a mealtime fantasy just isn't complete without a rich, chocolate dessert.

BLACK BOTTOM PIE

1 tablespoon unflavored gelatin
¼ cup cold water
2 ounces unsweetened chocolate
¾ cup sugar
1 tablespoon cornstarch
3 large eggs, separated
1¾ cups milk, scalded
1 tablespoon rum
¼ teaspoon salt
¼ teaspoon cream of tartar
¼ cup sugar
One 9-inch chocolate cookie crumb or ginger snap crust (see page 100)
½ cup heavy cream, whipped to firm peaks
Chocolate curls for decoration

In a small bowl, dissolve the gelatine in the water. In the top of a double boiler over simmering water, melt the chocolate.

Sift together ½ cup of the sugar and the cornstarch. In another saucepan, beat the egg yolks until light. Beat in the sugar-and-cornstarch mixture. Place over low heat, then slowly blend in the scalded milk, stirring constantly. Cook the mixture until thickened. Remove from the heat. Take out 1 cup of the custard.

Blend the melted chocolate into remaining custard. Pour into the pie crust and chill about 30 minutes.

Meanwhile, blend the dissolved gelatin into the reserved custard. Cool, then stir in the rum.

Beat the egg whites until frothy. Blend in the salt and cream of tartar. Gradually beat in the remaining sugar and continue beating until thick.

Blend together the egg and custard mixtures. Pour over the chocolate layer in the pie crust. Refrigerate at least 8 hours before serving.

Decorate the pie with the whipped cream and chocolate curls, if desired.

Your stale bread is no longer for the birds! Save it for this scrumptious bread pudding. If you do not have stale bread, toast fresh bread lightly.

BREAD PUDDING WITH WILD TURKEY SAUCE

10 slices stale bread or about 10 cups cubed
   loaf-style bread
2 large eggs
3 large eggs, separated
1 tablespoon pure vanilla extract
1½ teaspoons ground cinnamon
Pinch of salt
3 cups milk
1 cup sugar
2 tablespoons margarine or butter
1 cup raisins
Wild Turkey Sauce (see page 105)

Grease a 13- by 9-inch pan.

Break the bread into small pieces and place in the greased pan.

In a large bowl, blend the whole eggs into the egg yolks. Add the remaining ingredients, except the raisins, sauce, and egg whites. Beat the egg whites until stiff peaks form. Fold into the yolk mixture, then fold in the raisins.

Pour the mixture over the broken bread pieces. Bake in a preheated 350° F oven until the pudding is golden brown on top, 35 to 45 minutes.

Serve warm, topped with the sauce.

WILD TURKEY SAUCE

3 large eggs
1/4 cup sugar
1/2 teaspoon pure vanilla extract
1/4 cup (1/2 stick) butter, melted
1/4 cup Wild Turkey bourbon
1/2 cup milk, scalded

*I*n a heavy saucepan, beat the eggs. Add the sugar, vanilla, and butter, and cook over low heat until the mixture begins to thicken. Remove from the heat and stir in the bourbon. Beat in the milk until the sauce is creamy and very thick.

Rice is grown in many Southern states and used to delicious advantage in this simple dessert.

RICE PUDDING

½ teaspoon ground cinnamon
1 quart milk
1 cup uncooked long-grain rice
1 cup (2 sticks) butter
⅔ cup sugar
5 large eggs, beaten
1 teaspoon grated lemon rind
½ cup golden raisins
1 tablespoon pure vanilla extract

Grease a 13- by 9-inch baking dish and sprinkle with the cinnamon.

Bring the milk to a boil and add the rice. Reduce to low heat, stir once, cover, and cook until tender, about 15 minutes. Add the butter, sugar, eggs, lemon rind, raisins, and vanilla. Pour into the baking dish and bake in a preheated 350° F oven until pudding is set, 25 to 30 minutes.

Surprise! The crust rises from the bottom to the top in this peachy dessert.

FRESH PEACH COBBLER

½ cup (1 stick) margarine or butter
1 cup all-purpose flour
2 cups sugar
½ teaspoon salt
1 tablespoon baking powder
1 cup milk
3 cups peeled and sliced fresh peaches
1 teaspoon ground cinnamon
½ cup heavy cream, whipped to firm peaks, or
  vanilla ice cream (optional)

Melt the margarine in a 13- by 9-inch baking dish.

Sift together the flour, 1 cup of the sugar, the salt, and baking powder. Blend in the milk. Pour the mixture into the dish.

Toss the peaches with the remaining sugar and the cinnamon, then spread them on top of the crust mixture. Bake in a pre-heated 350° F oven until the crust rises and turns golden, about 1 hour.

Serve warm with the whipped cream or vanilla ice cream.

*Try this with McIntosh
or Cortland apples, or
with fresh peaches!*

APPLE DUMPLINGS

Pastry
2½ cups all-purpose flour
1 teaspoon sugar
1 teaspoon salt
½ cup vegetable shortening or unsalted butter,
   well chilled
1 large egg, slightly beaten
⅓ cup ice water

Apples
⅓ cup sugar
½ teaspoon ground cinnamon
⅛ teaspoon ground nutmeg
12 medium-size tart apples, peeled and cored
3 tablespoons butter

*T*o make the pastry, sift together the flour, sugar, and salt in a large bowl. Cut in the shortening with a pastry blender or 2 knives until the mixture resembles coarse crumbs. Add the egg and water, blending quickly with your fingers until the dough holds together. Press into a flat round and wrap in plastic wrap. Refrigerate 1 hour.

Roll out the dough on a lightly floured counter or board to a thickness of about ⅛ inch. Cut into twelve 8-inch squares.

Mix together the sugar, cinnamon, and nutmeg. Fill the hollowed core of each apple with some of the sugar mixture. Let stand for 15 minutes.

Place one apple on each of the 12 pastry squares. Dot the top of each apple core with some of the butter. Then fold the pastry up around the apples like a blanket. Pinch the seams together, leaving a hole at the top to allow steam to escape. Place in a baking dish and bake in a preheated 350° F oven until the pastry is golden and the apples are tender, 50 to 60 minutes.

Serve warm or at room temperature.

For peach dumplings, carefully halve 12 medium-size peaches and remove pits. Substitute for the apples, following the recipe for apple dumplings, but reduce the baking time to 30 to 40 minutes.

Benne *is the South Carolina word for sesame seed. Benne is used in crackers, but I favor these slightly sweet, crisp cookies.*

BENNE COOKIES

1 cup all-purpose flour
¼ teaspoon baking powder
½ teaspoon salt
½ cup vegetable shortening
1½ cups firmly packed brown sugar
2 large eggs, beaten until fluffy
1 teaspoon pure vanilla extract
1 cup toasted benne (sesame) seeds

Sift together the flour, baking powder, and salt.

In a large mixing bowl, beat the shortening until light and fluffy. Slowly add the sugar, beating well. Blend in the eggs and vanilla.

Add the flour mixture, stirring until thoroughly combined, then stir in the benne seeds.

Drop by teaspoonfuls onto a greased and floured baking sheet. Bake in a preheated 325° F oven until golden brown, 10 to 15 minutes. Store in an airtight container.

Makes about 2 dozen cookies.

To toast benne, spread seeds evenly on a cookie sheet or jelly roll pan. Then bake in preheated 350° F oven until golden, about 10 minutes.

I always think of Louisiana when I think of pralines, but these pecan candies are popular throughout the South.

PRALINES

2 cups firmly packed brown sugar
1 cup granulated sugar
1 cup heavy cream
1 cup water
3 cups broken pecans

Combine the sugars, cream, and water in a heavy saucepan and cook over medium heat to the soft ball stage (238° F on a candy thermometer), or when the sugar mixture forms a soft ball when plunged into ice water. Remove from the heat and beat until creamy, about 5 minutes. Add the nuts and drop by tablespoonfuls onto buttered, waxed paper. Cool completely.

Store in an airtight container.
Makes about 3 dozen cookies.

COOKIN' FOR THE MULTITUDES

BBQ PARTIES

Smoking generally requires much longer cooking times than traditional methods of cooking. This allows plenty of time for you to prepare accompaniments for your party. And best of all, barbecue is the perfect party food because it tastes as good at room temperature as it does hot. Whether cooking for your family or for a fanfare, barbecue is an exciting, tasteful way to go. Just make sure you allow more food for a barbecue than you would indoors. Appetites always seem heartier when smoke is in the air.

Being well organized is the key to a successful barbecue. Before starting, make sure you have marinades, sauces, and dry rubs on hand. Invest in a pair of quilted, insulated mitts to keep near your barbecue. Other utensils to keep nearby are a long-handled wooden or metal basting brush (do not attempt to use the short, plastic brushes), a long, flat spatula, a meat thermometer, and long tongs. Never use a fork to turn or remove meat.

The following are outlines for party menus and preparation suggestions which have worked well for parties we have catered. So get the fire started and happy smoking!

A SPECIAL FAMILY AFFAIR

*L*ightly spiced fried shrimp and okra are a great start for this meal—but not so heavy as to put a damper on the appetite.
Makes 6 servings.

Cajun Shrimp and Fried Okra with Special Tangy Sauce

Southern-Style Spare Ribs with Fast BBQ Sauce
Sweet 'n' Hot Baked Beans
Corn Pudding
Collard Greens

Chocolate Fudge Pecan Pie

1. The day before your party, prepare the Sweet 'n' Hot Baked Beans and Special Tangy Sauce; cover tightly with plastic wrap and refrigerate. Peel and devein the shrimp. Refrigerate in plastic or glass until ready to use.

2. Early the morning of your party (7 to 8 hours prior to the planned dinner time) prepare the smoker and bring the ribs to room temperature. Coat well with dry

rub. Place in the smoker and follow the recipe instructions.

3. Cut the okra and refrigerate in plastic or glass until ready to use; do not wash until ready to use.

4. Prepare and bake the Chocolate Fudge Pecan Pie. Store at room temperature until ready to serve. Refrigerating this pie will result in disaster unless you bring it to room temperature before dinner. It is so thick and fudgy that it is impossible to slice when cold.

5. About 2½ to 3 hours before dinner time, wash the collard greens well and let them drain slightly. Then put them in a large pot and begin cooking.

6. Two hours before dinner time, preheat the oven, prepare the corn pudding, and place it on the top rack of the oven. After it has been in the oven for 15 minutes, put the Sweet n' Hot Beans in, too.

7. Whip the cream for the pie, if desired.

8. Mix together the seasoned cracker meal and flour for the appetizers and set aside. Remove the ribs from the smoker and

tent loosely with aluminum foil. Heat the BBQ sauce.

9. About 40 minutes before you sit down to eat, heat the oil in the deep fryer. Fry the okra and, if necessary, hold in a slow oven at 200° F while frying the shrimp. Serve both immediately.

FOOD FOR A DOZEN FOLK

***D**ill* pickles and fried catfish go together like bees and honey. Serve the spicy sauce with the catfish. The pickles do not need an accompaniment. Finish with a not-too-sweet fruit dessert or two.

Fried Dill Pickles
Fried Catfish Fingers with Special Tangy Sauce

Pulled Pork with Pig Sauce
Bourbon Sweet Potatoes
Stewed Green Beans
Buttermilk Biscuits

Key Lime Pie and Peach Cobbler

1. The day before your party, prepare the Special Tangy Sauce, a double batch of Bourbon Sweet Potatoes, a double batch of Stewed Green Beans (adjust the seasonings but no need to increase the other ingredients except the beans), and the Key Lime Pie. Cover well and refrigerate.

2. The pork can also be smoked the day before, if desired, and shredded. To reheat the day of the party, heat the pig sauce to boiling. Turn off the heat and add the

shredded pork. Let the pork sit in the sauce 1 hour before serving.

3. On the afternoon of your party, mix the seasoned cornmeal for the catfish and set aside. Bring the sweet potato casserole to room temperature. Rinse the catfish and place in cold milk to soak at least 30 minutes before frying. If serving the Peach Cobbler, prepare it now.

4. One hour before your are ready to serve, preheat the oven to 350° F and bake the sweet pototoes, uncovered. Bake the cobbler at the same time. Meanwhile, prepare and cut the biscuit dough, placing them on ungreased baking sheets. Put the stewed green beans in a saucepan and warm over very low heat.

5. Twenty minutes before you sit down to eat, heat the oil in the deep fryer. Make the egg wash and set up the seasoned bread crumbs next to the wash.

6. Increase the oven temperature to 400° F. Remove the sweet potato casserole and cobbler from the oven. Deep fry the dill pickles and catfish, and drain well on paper towels. Place the biscuits in the oven to bake while you serve catfish and pickles.

A MIXED GRILL FOR FIFTY

*T*o serve a party of fifty means you'll have a whole lot of smokin' goin' on—but it'll be well worth your effort. Start a few days to a few weeks ahead of your party and things should go very smoothly. By using your oven and stove top, you will have plenty of room for re-heating.

Smoked Sausage over Black-Eyed Peas
Hush Puppies with Hot Pepper Sauce
Fried Onion Rings

Baby Back Ribs with Pepper Mint Jelly
Beef Brisket
Smoked Turkey Breast
Coleslaw
Horseradish Potatoes
Smothered Okra

Bread Pudding with Wild Turkey Sauce

1. Up to one week before the party, prepare dry rub for the turkey after lighting the smoker. Smoke a 10- to 12-pound turkey breast for 4½ to 6 hours, until a meat thermometer reaches 180° F. The breast will cook faster than a whole turkey. At the same time, smoke 10 pounds of sausage for the appetizer. Wrap tightly in

plastic wrap, then in aluminum foil, and refrigerate. When ready to serve, the turkey can be sliced and served cold or at room temperature. Prepare the Pepper Mint Jelly, if desired. This will keep 2 weeks if stored in a tightly covered container in the refrigerator. The sausage can be reheated by wrapping it tightly in aluminum foil and baking it in a preheated 350° F oven for 20 minutes. You can also grill or fry the sausage to heat through.

2. The black-eyed peas (6 pounds) and smothered okra (5 batches) can be prepared 1 to 3 weeks before the party and frozen, then thawed to room temperature and heated slowly over low heat on top of the stove. Prepare the Hot Pepper Sauce if you do not already have some on hand (shame on you!).

3. Three to 4 days before your party, make a triple batch of coleslaw and keep it refrigerated. Make a large batch of mashed potatoes by increasing the recipe to: 12 pounds potatoes, 3 sticks (¾ pound) margarine or butter, 1 tablespoon salt, 2 teaspoons freshly ground black pepper, 1½ cups cream-style horseradish, and 1 quart hot milk (give or take a little). Store in an airtight container in the refrigerator.

To reheat, spoon the potatoes into two greased 13- by 9- by 2-inch baking dishes, cover tightly with aluminum foil, and bake in a preheated 350° F oven for 30 minutes.

4. One to 2 days before the party, smoke 15 to 20 pounds of baby back ribs, brush with the mixture of vinegar and Pepper Mint Jelly (as mentioned in the Country-Style Ribs recipe), and cover tightly in plastic wrap and aluminum foil. When you're ready to serve, place the ribs on a baking sheet, coat them well again with the vinegar and mint jelly mixture, and heat in a preheated 350° F oven for 20 minutes. Do not overbake or they will become very dry.

5. The night before your party, smoke a 10- to 12-pound brisket. This will take approximately 14 to 16 hours, so have sweet dreams while your beef is cooking. Check the temperature of the meat first thing in the morning. It should be between 160° and 170° F before you remove the brisket from the smoker. The meat should be tender to the touch.

6. About 2½ hours before the party, prepare and bake 2 batches of Bread Pudding. Let

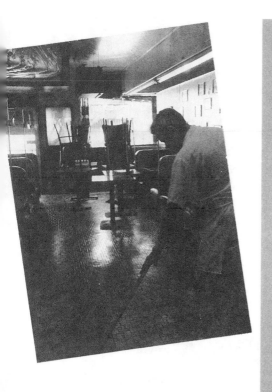

sit at room temperature until ready to serve. The whiskey sauce should be prepared just before dinner or prepared early, refrigerated, and then heated very slowly just before serving. The oven is now hot and ready for reheating the ribs and potatoes.

7. One to 1½ hours before your guests arrive, prepare 3 batches of Hush Puppy batter and 2 batches of Fried Onion Rings. As the guests begin to trail in, heat the oil in the deep fryer and cook fresh batches of hush puppies and onion rings to pass.

INDEX